Dear Kimberley,
   May your journey with the
Lord be rewarding, inspiring
and blessed.

I Tried To Tell You

Blanche Graves Williams

I Tried To Tell You

The Story of an Incredible Journey

BLANCHE GRAVES WILLIAMS

Cover concept by Juli Whitney.

ISBN: 1-58597-237-1

Library of Congress Control Number: 2003114623

A division of Squire Publishers, Inc.
4500 College Blvd.
Leawood, KS 66211
1/888/888-7696
www.leatherspublishing.com

Acknowledgments

Many thanks to so many:

- Reverend Everett Pendleton Williams, Sr., who supported me in everything I ever did.

- Theresa, Everett Jr. and Allen, three wonderfully talented and loving children.

- Marcheta and Willie, who joined the family as spouses of Theresa and Allen.

- Kamilah Madelyn, Meryl Ashley and Allen Louis the II, the grandchildren who became the joy of my later years.

- Dolores J. Cochrell, who listened to me recount stories of my travels and who said, "You need to write these stories down." She said, "You've done wonderful things and you need to share them."

- The book is especially dedicated to my sisters sharing in the pastoral life, even those who never wanted to be a minister's spouse.

- And thanks to Dr. Nevada Lee, who gave me the final "nudge," urging me to set a date for completion.

TABLE OF CONTENTS

INTRODUCTION

How It All Began

My family lived in Seattle, Washington at this time. My mother was born in Victoria, British Columbia, and had gone to Spokane, Washington to live with a friend of her mother and work. She met and married my dad, who was born in Moberly , Missouri.

Mother's name was Alice Beatrice Barnswell, and Daddy's was William Asa Graves.

We had lived in many homes and apartments, but when I was around ten or eleven years old we lived at 2610-1/2 E. Madison. Our apartment was above what used to be a store.

Dad was a chef, and a wonderful one, so he was away a lot.

I don't remember how we became acquainted with Brother John H. Carr, but he seemed to take to our family. He had been a Reverend, but was not actively pastoring when we met him.

He worked at the Security Public Market. On some Saturday evenings he would come and visit with us. He always brought goodies to eat, and it was like we had

My mom and dad, Bill and Bea Graves.

picnics or parties. He also brought us books. I loved to read, and I had a collection "to die for!"

He used to talk with us a lot, and we enjoyed his visits. As I look back, I really think he liked my mom. He was always a gentleman.

I was a very talkative girl from childhood on, and was told that when very young I would ask questions, and if no one answered me I would answer myself and keep on talking. Well, sometimes we would talk about what we wanted to do when we grew up, and Brother Carr said, I would say; "I want to be different." I believe I really meant that, and I think those words stuck in my mind and perhaps shaped the course of my life.

My family was somewhat worldly, lively and fond of fun-loving activities. They did some things I didn't like, so now I understand why I wanted to be different.

The lodge and dancing and card playing were important to them. But not me. People used to say things like, "I don't know where they got that child."

My brother, Billy Graves.

My Aunt Dorothy.

1

The Early Days in Seattle

VERY EARLY IN life I found joy and pleasure in the church. The Sunday school was very fascinating to me.

Another joy for me was taking care of small children. I often baby-sat. I was considered reliable. My parents let me use my earnings to buy small things I needed.

Those days in Seattle I could walk up to 23rd Avenue alone and care for children, and one of the parents would take me home at night. Later we moved to the nice house on E. John street, 2214. It was a white house and we liked it.

Our neighbors were Frances Chatters and her three boys, Gaynor, Merrit and George. They were cute and I loved them. I kept them sometimes. George called me (Glanche) and he would call me over the fence. He would say, "It's 'portant, Come now!" They were wonderful people.

On Sunday morning I would go by the home of the Hancocks and get Lyda Mae and also pick up Sonia M. Gamel. Sometimes they wouldn't be ready, but they would cry if I left them. I did this for a long time. We would walk all the way to 14th Street to First A.M.E. Church, and after Sunday school I would take them home.

My first friend was Barnetta Johnston. She had two brothers, James and Byron. Barnetta's mother, Alyce Johnston, and my dad, "Pretty Billy" Graves, were exceptional cooks, and we children had the very best of everything to eat.

My mom could cook, too, but mostly my dad did the honors. His specialty was hot rolls; apple and lemon pie, roasted suckling pig, complete with apple in the mouth. He originated a canned ham and sauce.

Mrs. Johnston could bake anything: spritz cookies, cakes (strawberry shortcake) and prune pie. They were a team.

My school friends were Marian Valley, Jean Shields, Clarine Garrett and Aura Bell Jackson. We went all the way from kindergarten to high school together. I stayed with them in Garfield High for a year and a half.

About this time, work got scarce for my dad, and he got a job in Portland, Oregon. He went ahead and got us a nice apartment (in a four-plex), and we joined him in June of 1939.

Life changed for all of us, and then I began to understand what it meant to "be different."

2

A New Life — Portland, Oregon

WHEN WE GOT to Portland, the family joined Bethel A.M.E. church. It was on McMillan Street, an old red brick church. Reverend George Martin was our pastor. This was remarkable because he had pastored us in Seattle. I remember him and his wife Myrtle especially because Reverend Martin buried my only sister in 1932. My sister, Beverly Joyce, was nine years old. She and a friend Voris Dawson were walking home from school, and as they passed by a grocery store an elderly lady lost control of her car and hit Beverly Joyce (Joy we called her). Voris was able to get away, but Joyce couldn't. She was taken to Harborview Hospital where she died two hours later. The nurses said, "Beverly, your mother's here." She said, "I know, I know." These were her last words.

The Martins did not stay long, and Reverends Browning C. Allen and Cornelius Austin Jr. followed them.

I loved the church and became very active. I was president of the Allen Christian Endeavor League, and I attended Sunday school and prayer meeting. I found the parsonage to be a haven, and I loved the Allens. They understood my desires and me.

I sang in the junior choir — because all the kids were in the choir. Bernice Williams was our director, and Helen Blanchard played for us. I couldn't sing, but no one cared. Our choir was so good; we had some of the Episcopalian kids singing with us.

Mrs. Allen was a fantastic cook and welcomed any of us to her table. Did we enjoy those evenings! Browning Jr.

hated to see me come by on the nights they had pork chops and macaroni and cheese. He often said, "Don't you have food at home?" That didn't stop me.

My best friends were Joyce Hilliard, Lurlene Gibbs, the Harrises, Juliet Hillard, Harriet (Dee) Fuller and Ila. I liked all the kids in the choir, but these were my close friends.

I didn't have a boyfriend, but Browning Jr. and Louis Fuller teased me a lot. The Hilliards lived on the southeast side of town, and they had to take the streetcar to get to Bethel.

Again, my love for children was a big item with me. My pets were Mary Ann Fuller, Charmaine Blanchard and Patsy Anderson. I would take them places and they loved it. Patsy's mother was a beautician and sometimes did my hair.

When there were parties, the "nice kids" could go if I was going. This worked pretty well, even though the "parties" changed dramatically after my departure, I am told.

Shortly after the Allen family arrived in Portland, Florence Hildebrand, their "adopted" foster daughter came to live with them. Florence had a magnificent voice and used to sing on Sundays before Reverend Allen preached, "Remember me." Speaking of singing, I'll always remember Jimmie Allen taking the solo part in "Every Time I feel the Spirit." He was utterly "cool."

Florence and I became good friends. Florence told me often that one day she hoped to have a daughter, a smart daughter. Later in life, God blessed her with Paula, a real smart child.

Later that year, a representative of the Methodist Church came to talk with Reverend and Mrs. Allen to request their help in finding a black (we were "Negroes" then) girl to send to Bennett College as a project they had. Bennett was a Methodist School for women and at that time was considered the "Vassar of the South," an academic finishing school.

The Allens thought of me and suggested my name. I said, "I'll think about it," and Mrs. Allen in her decisive way said, "What's there to think about? You want to go to college? Here's a way." I said yes, but the biggest problem I had was with my dad and mother.

3

A Bold Decision

LOOKING BACK, I can understand my parents' hesitance on my going to Bennett. I was born and reared in the Pacific Northwest. All we knew of the South were tales we had heard. I'm sure my folks thought of the distance between Oregon and North Carolina. I'm sure they thought of my safety as I traveled alone. I'm sure they had mental pictures of "colored only" places, real segregation. Mom was born and reared in Victoria, British Columbia. Her family was interracial. I can imagine her fears for me. What did I know? Only that " I wanted to be different." Already I had disappointed them by not being interested in Eastern Stars, Politics (Dad was an active Republican, and Mom said he could find a job for anybody but himself). Mom was very witty and full of fun.

Maggie Shepherd was the first girl from Portland to go to Bennett on this Methodist Scholarship, and I would be the second.

4

Challenges

I HAD A wonderful talk with the representative from the Methodist Church. They would pay my tuition, board and room and allowance for incidentals. I was only asked to do my best. I was on my way. I was sure that this was in God's plan for me.

I won my parents over. They knew that they would not have been able to send me to school.

I was a mid-year graduate and had to work until the beginning of the regular school year.

There was an elite cleaning establishment called "Dave Levine's Cleaners." It was near downtown Portland, and I had to take two streetcars to get there. A young black man had the job of meeting cars and receiving their laundry (shirts) and cleaning and taking clothes that were finished to their cars. The young man was leaving, and I applied for the job. I was told that I couldn't handle the job- it was too hard for a girl. I could get hurt trying to cross the street, and I couldn't reach the racks. I stood my ground and got the job. It lasted until I graduated from Bennett. I made $13 a week. I wore a green suit with a cap to match. People were kind to me, and the tips were good. So good that Mr. Levine stopped them and gave me a raise; now I earned $14 a week. He let me work each year as soon as I came home for the summer. The other employees took an interest in me. Some of them gave me their daughter's gently used clothes so that I would have clothes for college. My other friend, Lurlene Gibbs, gave me her clothes, too, and I felt as good as any other girl at Bennett.

Reverend Allen used to say, "God has his hands on you," and surely this was true.

I did not remember anyone else in my school years going to college on a four-year scholarship.

5

The Bennett Years

HIGH SCHOOL FOR me was just a step you had take, and I was definitely an average student. My mother did all she could to help me.

It was during my high school years in Portland that I acquired the nickname "Blanco." We were in Spanish class, and Louis Fuller called me that and it stands today.

Bennett was truly a grand and glorious experience. I studied hard. I had my first black teacher. My name was on the Honor Roll every semester. My teachers let me know that I was a "student," and if I didn't do well they would fail me.

As a junior, I was president of my class. I graduated in the top five!

6

The Real Thing

AFTER THE FIRST year, I came home and went back to work for Dave Levine. I resumed my activities in the church. It was time for a "young people's" meeting in Spokane, Washington. It must have been a Sunday school convention. I was elected a delegate to go. We were going on the train. When I asked Mr. Levine to let me off, he said no. I was devastated and I went into the room where clothes were kept and cried as if my heart would break. After a few minutes, Mr. Levine told one of the female workers, "She's serious about that church meeting, and I had better let her go."

We all had fun on the train. As soon as we all got settled, Reverend Allen suggested that we eat! Mrs. Allen had prepared the lunch, and it was special.

That evening, we went to the church for a welcome program. (Some of us girls stayed in the parsonage.) On the program to sing was a young minister, Reverend Everett P. Williams. I can't remember what he sang, but I'll always remember him. This was the same Everett Williams that Alyce Johnston told me I should meet, the same Everett P. Williams that she told, "You should meet Blanche Graves. " Of course, we made it a point to try not to meet.

Florence Hildebrand was sitting next to me, and I remember telling her, "I'm going to marry him." Then and there I knew I wanted to marry a minister. I wanted the kind of life ministry would provide, and God told me that this was the preacher I would marry.

Years later, his theme song was going to be, "If this

isn't love, it'll have to do 'til the real thing comes along."

Florence and I began planning our strategy, and we asked Reverend Allen if he would invite Everett to preach at Bethel.

Of course, he said he would and he did. When we learned he was coming, Florence told me to ask my mother if I could spend the night with her. My mom said, "Well, you don't walk in your sleep, so you can."

On Sunday he preached on the subject, "Stairway to Heaven." I don't even remember what he sang, but I do know it got to me.

Joyce Hilliard had left us for California and was being courted by Franklin Williams, whom she later married, and her younger sister Juliet and I had formed a friendship that still exists.

7

Love Fulfilled

I WENT BACK to school, and for over a year Everett and I kept up a wonderful correspondence. We weren't able to see each other much, but we managed to get engaged. We planned to marry at the end of my junior year, but I felt I owed the Methodist church something. They told me I could marry and still finish school because I had been faithful and did very well. Even though my heart told me that I could, my head told me to hold off.

My parents again were not thrilled with my choice of a life partner. Dad wanted me to let him find me a job, and Mom just wanted me home.

Finally, after graduation, Everett let me know how much he loved me and said, "I'm going to Kansas to attend Seminary at Western University, in Quindaro Kansas, and I'm going with or without a wife!" That was one ultimatum I understood. I said, "Yes, I'll go with you."

8

Marriage

MY PARENTS WERE against the whole idea. They would be losing me again, they thought. I later learned that Mom didn't think that I was strong enough for the ministry.

They didn't go all out for a church wedding, although the members of Bethel felt I had earned it and they were willing to do everything. I said, "No, this should be my parents' job ,and if they didn't want to do it, we would just be married in the parsonage."

Reverend and Mrs. Allen had been transferred to southern California, and Reverend and Mrs. C.N. Austin Jr. were pastoring Bethel.

The Austins were a wonderful young couple with five beautiful children. They let me baby-sit for them, and we got along well.

So we planned a quiet wedding in the parsonage, and I accepted the offer of the church members to do the reception.

Up to the last moment we did not know whether or not my parents would come, but they did come. The eventful date was August 24, 1946.

My dear friend Juliet was supposed to be my only attendant. She worked for Dr. Unthank, a very dear gentleman. His wife Thelma also worked in the office, and she decided at the last minute not to let Juliet off. She was very sorry, but she had to work. Benny Gragg, who was the next Bennett Belle, stepped in at the last minute, and we were grateful.

Lurlene Gibbs, who had a lovely voice, sang for us, and

we had a beautiful wedding. Reverend Austin did a nice job.

While I was waiting to go downstairs for the ceremony, Carol, then five years old, gave me some very good advice. She said, "I hope you don't have too many children like my mother has." There were five little Austins. Many years later, at my 50th anniversary, I had the pleasure of reminding her of her advice as I laughingly reminded her that she did very well with her eight children.

When Reverend Austin pronounced us "Man and Wife," we embarked on the "Incredible Journey" that was to last for 54 years, ending when Everett drew his last breath on April 17, 2001.

We spent our first night in the home of Mr. and Mrs. Locke.

9

Seminary Days

EVERETT HAD AN old, but reliable car. His best man, James Monroe Moore, wanted to go to his home in Statesville, North Carolina, so he accompanied us on what was a combination honeymoon and drive to Kansas City to begin our new life.

Moore and Everett took turns driving and sat in the front seat, and I sat in the back with some of the luggage.

We stopped in San Francisco to see the late Reverend and Mrs. Chester Toliver.

We stopped in Los Angeles with our beloved friends, Reverend and Mrs. B.C. Allen. Florence was married to Ike Woods and was very happy. We had a good time. Moore left us here.

Our next stop was with Reverend and Mrs. Hayes in Kansas City, Missouri. Reverend Hayes had been Everett's pastor in Seattle, Washington, while he was attending school. Reverend Hayes asked us to stay there and take over his youth work. Everett declined, saying he had come to Kansas to go to school.

Everett went to Western University in Quindaro, Kansas. The building in which we lived was never intended for dormitory life. We had two rooms, one where we had a hot plate and a window box to keep food in. We shared it with the mice. The other room was one with a bed where we mostly lived.

Everett was a real student and did exceptionally well. This was a three-year program, but it turned out that he finished in one year.

In this same building we had good neighbors; Reverend Melvin Simmons and his wife Pauline, Reverend Henry Cummings and his wife, Reverend Elliot Scott and his wife Julia, and Reverend Roy Morris and his wife Lorene.

The Scotts and Cummings had stoves, and once in a while they let us cook something.

10

Our First Church Together

EVERETT GOT A church to pastor, Saint Paul, Olathe. Reverend Simmons got Paola. We sometimes drove together.

My sisters and brothers serving as ministers' spouses today would have been appalled at our living conditions,. In fact, they would never have crossed the threshold of that old creaky and cold building. Some of the older wives in the nearby churches gave us canned goods. Some of our churches gave us food.

Often we just received enough cash to get back home, and we trusted God to get us back on Sundays.

I truly understand the meaning of certain lines from the marriage vows, especially "in sickness and in health." Everett was put to the test early on, and did he ever measure up!

We had no health insurance, but God did provide. Dr. C.W. Alexander was my doctor, and he discovered a tumor. Douglas Hospital was a part of our campus, but you needed insurance to get in. Reverend George Martin, L.R. Hayes and T.J. Burwell worked together and got me in. I thanked God. The tumor turned out to be a cyst, and while treating that, they felt it wise to take out my appendix.

Everett had a job to supplement what the church gave us, and he also took care of me. He was wonderful.

I had cousins (they were second cousins to my grandmother, Martha Robinson). They were the Jackson girls, Minnie, Nellie, Eva and Marietta. They were kind and made every effort to assist us.

I knew nothing about cooking, house keeping, laundry, etc. Everett was loving and patient. He had what was then called "a nervous stomach," so our food choices were very limited. This condition was to plague him the rest of his life. At age 16, he and his twin brother Edward were without parents present because they had passed away. And when their grandparents who reared them passed away, they were on their own.

Both twins were gifted singers and both had learned to play an instrument.

They gave a concert later to raise money to go to school. There wasn't enough for both, so they worked it out that Ed would go to Fisk, and when he finished, Everett would go.

God was in the plan, and Everett stayed in Seattle, Washington. Everett went to school there.

We met and now you have the story of how we got together, became engaged and married!

11

Meeting Everett's Twin Brother and Family

WELL, ED AND Everett hadn't seen each other in a long time. Ed was pastoring in Danville, Kentucky, and he wanted to see Everett, so we bussed to Kentucky and spent our first Christmas with Ed and his family.

Ed was married to a very, very lovely lady named Mattie Belle Pride. She was truly a Christian lady. She was a schoolteacher. They had two of the cutest children I

Everett Sr., the twin who made the journey.

Edward P. Williams, Everett's twin brother.

had ever seen. The boy was named Edward P. Williams, Jr., and the girl was named Gwendolyn Ann. E.P. Jr. couldn't say Gwendolyn, and so he just said "Babee," and to this day we still call her Babee. Mattie was also rearing her younger sister, Ruth, who had been with her since she was about three years old, when their mother died.

We had a most enjoyable visit. The twins were mischievous still, and had a good time fooling people who got them mixed up. Mattie and I formed a friendship that lasted until the day that God called her home.

We went back to Kansas City and the church at Olathe.

The church had a parsonage! But it had an "out-house." I had never seen an "out-house" before! Inside the parsonage was a potbellied stove to heat it up.

One of the couples in the church was Eugene and Flora Jenkins. I think they sensed my dismay, and they welcomed us into their home. We only stayed on weekends, and it proved to be a good arrangement.

I was blessed to have a good recovery from the surgery I had in February.

12

For Better, For Worse;
In Sickness and In Health

VERY SHORTLY AFTER that I became pregnant. What did I know about having babies? Nothing!

Reverend Burwell's wife was a nurse, and she told me that I should not have become pregnant so soon after surgery. She said, "You have nothing to give a child." She was right.

Shortly after her warning to me, I was back in Douglas hospital experiencing a miscarriage. Pauline Simmons was in the same hospital celebrating the birth of her first child, Gwendolyn Ouida. I remember they let us have a meal together.

These were sad days for me. Then, one very hot July day, I got ill and had to be taken back to the hospital. Upon serious reflection I am convinced that the second visit to the hospital was the miscarriage of the second baby, indicating that I had been pregnant with twins. Dr. Alexander was on vacation, so Dr. Dyer waited on me. My relatives offered to take me home when Dr. Dyer was ready to release me. But he said, "No, she should be with her husband."

Again, Everett stepped up to the plate. I remember that he actually carried me up the stairs to our apartment.

He was wonderful! He had to work, but he prepared everything I needed right there by my bedside, because I couldn't get very far.

One thing he had decided was that I could not go through this again, and he said, "We will have no children." Secretly I cried many days. He did not know that I was praying and asking God to please let me have a baby!

Eventually I got my strength back. We had hoped my mother would have been able to help care for me, but Kansas City was very hot and she couldn't stand the heat. But God had provided me with a wonderful husband who stood by me in every way. We made it.

13

A New Pastorate and
New Opportunities for Everett

WHEN CONFERENCE CAME, Everett was appointed to Ward, Iola, Kansas.

We encountered many challenges there. Bishop Noah W. Williams was our Bishop at that time. Bishop Williams had become elderly and was possibly senile, and at conference he appointed another pastor to Iola and not us. Our experienced friends said, "Everett, go on to Iola now." The minister who was there did not want to leave, but again, God was in the plan and we were able to get in.

My parents both came to visit us there. They came separately according to their own timetables.

The parsonage had no bathroom in the house, and so I learned about the old tin tub! The kitchen did not have a modern sink! When my dad came, he literally drew us a plan showing us how we could get a nice bathroom and a kitchen sink.

With God's help and a positive membership, we were able to reach that goal.

No more would Everett have to empty the "old chamber" each day! He didn't have to, but he did it for me. Here was another test of his love for me.

14

The Twins Were Together Again

ABOUT THIS TIME Edward learned of a vacancy in the 13th District under Bishop R.R. Wright. The church in Richmond, Kentucky was open and we could have it.

I knew how much the twins longed to be near each other, and so we said good-bye to the 5th District and went to Richmond.

When we arrived in Richmond, we were taken to the parsonage. A lady who lived in another town owned the house. She kept a room there, of course, locked up.

The ladies who showed us the house came bringing food for us. As one of the ladies left, she said "There's a rat in here." She was telling me the truth; there was a rat in the house and I was afraid.

We spent the night, and the next morning we found potatoes from our kitchen in the hall near the bathroom. The rats had done that.

If ever there was a time when I longed for my family home on McMillan St., this was it.

Everett said he didn't want me to go because he loved me. We went to the hardware store and bought tin shears. He cut cans and covered up all the holes he could find. He worked so hard to make the house livable. What a wonderful man I had married!

My college friend, Theresa Neely from Detroit, came to visit us there and helped me learn a lesson I never forgot. Wherever we were sent, I would have to take beauty and contentment with me. I knew that God would meet us there and we survived.

We were told that if we saw one or two rats that meant that there were many under the house. We had to open the landlord's room to help us assess the extent of the rat situation. From the landlord's room we found more rats under the floorboards. From there we went to work to rid our home of the rats.

On the streets in Kentucky you could see rats holding Coca Cola bottles.

Everett and I exercised our faith that God would take care of us, and He did.

I still longed to have a baby and began seeing a doctor to find out if it would be possible. Everett joined me in wanting a family now.

While the doctor was working with me, God intervened and I became pregnant. It was definitely His plan.

While the congregation was very good to us I longed for an environment I knew. My father really wanted to see us come back to the Fifth district and actually talked to the Bishop.

15

Back to the Fifth —Yakima, Washington

AN OPENING CAME in Yakima, Washington, and we learned that we could have it. I was thrilled because I was afraid to have my baby in the segregated hospital in an isolated area.

The members of the church were saddened at our leaving, but they understood. Some said to let them know when the baby was born, and they did send gifts. I really was glad that through faith and love we stayed as long as we did and left a loving congregation.

Bethel, Yakima proved to be a marvelous experience. The congregation was most congenial and we enjoyed them.

There had not been a baby born to that congregation in 28 years, and so enthusiasm was high. We had lots of elderly ladies in the church, and so I received lots of advice.

My obstetrician was a Frenchman who was very competent. He could tell that I didn't know much about babies, so he had me take a class on child-care. That class really helped me.

Our church had a great men's chorus and a wonderful Sunday school. The teachers used to meet often, and we met in homes over breakfast. We had a good time.

Our Missionary Society was large, and most of the time we were served big dinners. My mother was visiting us one time, and I said, "They always serve dinner, so we don't need to have dinner at home." We were ready for that! When we got to the home of the hostess, we could see no signs nor smell anything that resembled dinner. The group was large and at the appropriate time, the hostess brought out some ice cream and gingerbread! I don't need to tell you what my mom said when we got home! My mother was there because the doctor had said my baby would be born December 12th. My dad joined us and we all waited. It became apparent that my time had been off, so my parents went home thinking the baby would come January 12th.

Well, babies do their own thing, and on Sunday, January 1, 1950, Alyce Theresa Williams arrived. She was beautiful! Some of the Caucasian ministers came around to see the beautiful black baby girl that they had heard about.

The church had given us a bountiful baby shower, and we didn't have to buy anything.

We were grateful to God for our new daughter and truly welcomed her into our home. Everett was very good with her, and I knew that he would be an excellent father.

Life was wonderful, and we couldn't ask for more. Our work was flourishing.

I was reminded that God often gives us over and abundantly more than we ask, and sure enough, I soon discovered I was pregnant again and this baby would be born before the year was out!

Two babies in one year. Our children were born before the technology would be common, allowing you to know for sure the sex of your child, so we waited on God. And He truly blessed us again.

Our little son, Everett Pendleton Williams, Jr., was born December 16, 1950. What a blessing!

Theresa was very cooperative and did all the things you would expect a baby to do, and so caring for two children was not hard.

We had lots of help. The young people liked to come by and take Theresa to the church, which was just next door. Then I would bring the baby.

Although today the practice is to live away from the

church, at that time you lived very close to church. In some instances the parsonage was even connected to the church.

We had a wood and coal stove, which I never learned to use. Everett made the fires. In fact, Everett did everything around the house. I cooked and did major things for the babies. He got up at night and always seemed to know what they needed or wanted. In Everett, I had a treasure and I knew it.

I think all that Everett wanted outside of his pastoring was a home and family, and I was determined to see that he got it.

16

California — Here We Come!

WE SPENT TWO years in Yakima. Everett had the vision to know when his work was done and when he should move on. And God always met us where we landed.

He wrote to the late Bishop D. Ormonde Walker and told him of his desire to move. Bishop Walker was not happy, but sent us to southern California where we were to meet him.

We were at breakfast with the Bishop and his wife. Mrs. Walker, with concern, said, "These children have nowhere to go."

One of the openings was in Ogden, Utah, and one was in Tulare, California.

We were staying in Los Angeles with Reverend and Mrs. Allen.

Jimmie Allen, the son of Reverend and Mrs. Allen, was home at that time, and he took Everett to check out Tulare and decided that that would be the best place for us to land.

The Bishop gave him the appointment and we went. The church, Brooks Chapel, was in the process of building a parsonage, but it was not finished. Commuting to Los Angeles was difficult.

One of the members had a home with an extra building that could serve as a guest house. It was really too small, so we ended up staying in their home. We were all happy when the new parsonage became livable. There's nothing like your own place. "Amen."

17

My First Job Since College

THE CHURCH IN Tulare was small and could only afford to pay us about $25 a week. With our family of four; Everett, Blanche, Theresa and Everett, Jr., we realized that one of us would have to work.

When it became apparent that the new "preacher's wife" had a college degree, an offer of employment became a reality. While we were looking at our options, Everett and I agreed that the first one to get a job would take it, and the other one would take care of the children.

God surely does provide. There was an all black community, Allensworth, located almost in Kern County, near Bakersfield. A former resident, Alwortha Tompkins, came home to be the principal of the one-room school. She needed someone to teach kindergarten through fourth grade. I had graduated from Bennett with a major in Sociology and a minor in Social Science. Everyone took Educational Psychology, and that was as near as I got to "Education." On sheer faith and overwhelming support of my beloved husband, I accepted.

Before the term "house-husband" had ever been used, Everett stepped up to the plate.

I could not drive, and it was about 35 miles up 99 Highway and then about 12 miles off the interstate to Allensworth.

Everett took me out one day to teach me to drive and after one try, immediately got one of our members, Zora Scott, to try to do the impossible, teach me to drive. The very first try, I got us stuck in the mud, and Zora had to call her husband, Raymond, to come and get us out.

The day I went to get my first license, the examiner sad, "It's up to you." I made it.

The children were in very good hands. Everett Sr. planned the very first children's lunchtime diet, vanilla or chocolate pudding and peanut butter sandwiches. You should hear their version!

Until I could make the drive alone, we dressed the children and he drove me to work, went back home and then came back at the end of the school day and drove us back home.

My very first paycheck was primarily used to pay the Standard Oil gasoline bill.

I had always loved to talk. My mother had told me that when I was very young I talked all the time. She said that I would ask questions and that if no one was paying attention, I would answer myself and kept right on talking.

My first experience at speaking came when one of the ladies in the Methodist church invited me to speak at a function a few miles from Portland. Juliet went along with me.

The audience was very appreciative. I talked about Bennett College. It was easy, because I loved school and had done well.

One summer when I came home, I was asked to speak at Bethel A.M.E. Church. My subject was "The Four Wishes," and I will never forget it, because one man joined the church. The Stewards had invited me, because the pastor was away.

After my marriage, I was asked to speak at every church Everett pastored. He was so encouraging and really listened to me. I enjoyed it so much, and to this day I have kept every message I gave. I knew that God had given me this gift, and I used it freely.

We stayed in Tulare two years. After being at Allensworth one semester, the principal of Lincoln Elemen-

I enjoyed speaking at every church we pastored — especially for Missionary Day and Women's Day.

tary School, which was located just a stone's throw from our home, stopped by our house and asked me if I wouldn't like to teach closer to home. His name was James Arieda, and he didn't have to ask me twice!

There was an opening in the fifth grade because the teacher there, although well prepared, wasn't able to do the job. Here I was a neophyte, with very little experience, on a provisional credential. Everett told me I should do it, and so did my brother-in-law, Edward. Again, I set out in faith and managed to stay there until school closed.

One day the superintendent of schools was visiting the school and came into my classroom. He told me afterward that I should go back to school and get my credential. He said I would make a fine teacher. God leads us where He wants us to go, and I had faith enough to try.

I took the first step right where I was and took a course

at an extension class from Fresno State right there in Tulare.

We were sent to Stockton, California, and there we faced many challenges. We actually stayed there for five years. During those years Everett did a great job.

The parsonage was in skid row, and the church was right next door. In fact, the men used a bathroom at the back of our house.

As he had always done, Everett did a great job of making the house livable.

We realized that we needed to do something to make sure Theresa and Everett, Jr. had some place to play, so I took a temporary job in a beauty salon at one of the department stores, so we could put them in day care.

In the mean time, my dad came to visit us. One afternoon, he decided to take a walk, and in just a few minutes he was back in the house. He was very upset because he saw the winos sleeping under porches and in the street. (Of course, he was urging us to move).

Soon we were able to move into Edison Villa, an acceptable project community.

I was able to get into the school system. I continued taking classes and eventually received my regular credential and went on to get a Life Diploma with the State of California.

Everett and the congregation of Ebenezer A.M.E. Church worked together and moved them to the church that they still occupy in downtown Stockton.

God blessed us to purchase our first home. Perhaps the biggest blessing we had was the newest and last addition to our family, Allen Louis Williams, born on January 14th, 1956.

Theresa and Everett Jr. were very calm, obedient children. It seemed they did everything they were supposed to do, when they were supposed to do it! In my mother's words concerning Allen, "Now you have a real baby."

FORM J-8-A TULARE COUNTY REVISION.
CALIF. STATE DEPT. OF EDUCATION

TULARE COUNTY SCHOOLS
SCHOOL DISTRICT CONTRACT
Offer of Employment

Mrs. Blanche Williams _____ Allensworth _____, California

901 South F St. _____ December 3 _____ 19 51

Tulare, California _____

You are hereby notified that at a meeting of the Governing Board of **Allensworth**

School _____ District, held **December 3** _____ 19 **51** you were elected to

serve as a ~~full time~~ **teacher** _____ for the school beginning July 1, 19 **51** and
(position)

ending June 30, 19 **51** _____

The following conditions of employment have been stipulated by the Governing Board and are hereby expressly made a part of this contract:

1. Your annual salary for the school year in the above named position will be $ **1,876.88** _____, payable as follows:

   $196.88 on January 1, 1952 and 280 dollars on the first of each succeeding

   month to July 1, 1952.

2. Your services in the above named position will begin **December 3,** _____ 19 **51**

3. You will be required to render service in the above named position for such length of time during the school year as the Governing Board of the School District may direct.

4. You are hereby classified by this Board as a **probationary** employee, subject to acceptance of this offer.

5. The Governing Board reserves the right to revise upward from time to time during the year the salary stated on this contract, provided that in the opinion of the Board, living conditions and costs make such action advisable, and provided further that funds are available.

6. This offer of employment is made subject to the laws of California and to the lawful rules of the State Board of Education and of the Governing Board of the above named School District affecting the terms and conditions of employment of Governing Boards of School Districts. Said laws and rules are hereby made a part of the terms and conditions of this offer of employment, the same as though they had been expressly set forth herein.

(Signed) _Walter Nelson_
Member

Emery T Booth _____
Clerk/Secretary

Eric Clark
Member

ACCEPTANCE OF OFFER

I accept the above offer of employment and the terms and conditions thereof and will report for duty as directed. I hold and have on file or registered in the office of the Tulare County Superintendent of Schools the following credentials or certificates authorizing me to serve in the capacity stipulated in this contract:

Date of Birth _October 14, 1823_ Date _December 14_ 19 51

Number of Income Exemptions _2_

Annuity Percentage _____ (Signed) _Mrs. Blanche Williams_

P.A. Form 244A

34

If you talked to our very dear friend, Muriel James, she would tell you, "Blanche, he cries every day." It didn't seem to matter the condition he was in, whether wet, dry, hungry or full, for about ten months, he just cried! He too was a beautiful, healthy child. He was active, active, active, but he was a joy.

Allen hung out with his dad while the older ones were in school.

In school, a standard activity seemed to be to tell the class what your parents did.

Both Theresa and Everett Jr. would answer like this, "He waxes the floor, washes the dishes, sets the table, washes the clothes, makes the beds and takes care of the baby." It never occurred to them that he was a minister, pastored a church and was very active in the community. Their Aunt Mattie, our sister-in-law, said. "I'm going to see to it that Allen understands this when his turn comes to tell people what his daddy does.

Muriel James and sons Donald and Dennis James — we've been friends for more than 40 years!

18

Our Outreach

THEY NEVER HAD any trouble telling what Mommy did! She teaches school.

Everett was so supportive of my willingness to help out financially. We were able to help other young people in a financial way to help them to go to college and realize their goals.

As I look back. I think of Donna Mae Johnson. Her mother was rearing Donna, her sister Lucille and her two brothers alone. Donna had great potential and became a wonderful teacher.

She met Aster Page, a fine Christian young man. He worked in the Sheriff's Department and was a part of a wonderful family. Everett married them, and they became like our own children. They eventually had two children, Gregory Tyrone and Danita Lynn.

We made many friends in Stockton. Among those cherished were J.C. and Alsester Craig. Alsester was only 13 when she married J.C. They loved the children, and Alsester was asked to be Allen's godmother. J.C. and Alsester used to keep them sometimes, and J.C. would tell them stories.

Later, Alsester's mother, Mrs. Scott, became Allen's baby sitter. There was nothing she did not know about children, as she was the mother of 17.

19

Grandma Robinson Joins Us

MY GRANDMOTHER, MARTHA Robinson, my dad's mother, wanted to visit my mom and dad and stay awhile, but my mother said, "You should go and visit Everett and Blanche. You'll have more fun." She came and stayed quite a while. We enjoyed her. She taught me much about life. Every Saturday she made hot rolls. I made applesauce, and you could forget the rest of my cooking! Grandma Robinson was queen of the kitchen, and the children were delighted.

She loved to cook and iron, and we urged her to do whatever she liked. She and Allen sometimes traveled with Everett.

I was teaching on what was called staggered sessions, and so my hours were late morning until late afternoon. It was good having Grandma Robinson there.

One of the things that made our home beautiful was our habit of sharing; Everett and I enjoyed sharing. There was no "his and hers," it was always "ours." Everett was able to now devote all of his time to pastoring, and he worked at home in childcare and housework. He loved it and I had sense enough to appreciate his abilities. He and his brother had been taught by their grandfather to work, and they took pride in a job well done.

Our house was well kept, and he was definitely the best of the best housekeepers.

On my paydays he would come to my classroom and pick up my paycheck and deposit it and take care of our business. He made very sure that the children knew that we could not have all the things we had if Mama didn't work.

When I would get home on payday, we would go to special places to have dinner. We wanted them to appreciate some of the finer things of life. It took a very long time to get them to stop ordering hamburgers on Fisherman's Wharf. It "hurt" a little to pay a huge price for a burger that wasn't at all "like" McDonald's. We did have fun though.

20

Changes, Changes, Changes

AFTER FIVE YEARS there, Bishop R.R. Wright was sent to the Fifth District. He approached Everett and told him that he wanted to appoint him as Presiding Elder of the Oakland, Sacramento District. Everett really did not want to be a Presiding Elder. The Bishop said, "All right, and that he wouldn't appoint him." When the appointments were read, Bishop Wright called his name as the Presiding Elder of the Oakland, Sacramento District. We were not overjoyed, but Everett was obedient and trusted God. He served one year.

That was a year that I will always remember. Sometimes he took Allen with him, and the people on the District really spoiled our little guy.

About this time, a new Bishop, Bishop Thomas Primm, took Everett off the District and sent him to St. Paul, Berkeley.

21

A New Church and a New Home!

IT WAS NICE. I substitute taught for a long time. Things had changed, and I felt that I needed to see how schools were faring. God had other plans for me.

Allen was a very active child, and it seemed wise for me to stay at home and care for him myself.

The new church required Everett to be available much more, and we worked together to make it possible. God is good, and we learned that if you trust Him He does provide. This was a lesson that really helped us in each step we took.

We became active in the Minister's Wives Alliance (men joined, too!) and everyone liked to come to our house. There were several of us who had families; The Kellers, the J. Russell Browns, the Habershams, the Devereauxs, the Andersons (Earl and Arsie), and what a time we had. The Halls (Preacher and Helen) didn't have children, but they loved ours. Sol and Tessie Hill with their sons were around also.

During this time my brother, Billy, showed up, and we were able to stay in touch until he passed away in the middle 1990s.

I continued speaking whenever asked and enjoyed it. I worked on the Conference Branch Women's Missionary Society, as well as the Local and Area Branches.

Eventually, I went back to work.

22

An Unusual Situation

EVERETT WAS SENT from St. Paul, over to Parks Chapel, Oakland. It was unusual because it was only a few steps away from St. Paul. Only a street or two separated Berkeley and Oakland.

Parks Chapel offered a real challenge for Everett. We worked very hard there. Everett could really preach, and his singing enhanced his services.

While we were in this area, we added to our extended family. Mary Julia Gary was known as "Aunt Mary Julia" to all three of our children. I know that God sent her to become an angel in our household. If you wanted to get a stern rebuff, just say something negative about the Williams family to Mary Julia. She was faithful in her devotion to us.

We were blessed to be near Everett's twin brother Edward a good bit now. His children were in and out of the area.

The Casson family became like family to us also. Their baby, Helen Madeline, became our goddaughter. Ellis worked with Everett in the church.

Going back to the church, Parks Chapel was in downtown Oakland, and was in the line of the soon-to-be needed part of urban development. We had been successful in securing a lovely parsonage for them, and now they needed a church home.

The logical place for relocation was East Oakland. Even the members of the church who were moving from West Oakland were moving east.

The church as a whole did not welcome the idea of going to East Oakland. As I look back on it, roots go deep, and Parks Chapel had many people who had been there for years, and they just were not going to East Oakland.

The church got over $100,000, and Everett made a decision which I believe few pastors could do. The decision was to leave the money there and not to build the church in East Oakland. He knew what the best plan would be, and the choice they wanted to accept was not wise. So he asked the Bishop to allow him to leave, and he decided to go back to Seattle, to Seattle Pacific University and complete some studies he had not been able to do before. The children and I remained in Oakland until the end of the school semester.

At this time it was the right thing to do, for families to be together, and so when my semester break came, the family became one again and we began a new life in Seattle. Everett Jr., Theresa and Allen were good troopers and adjusted. Everybody was in school except me, so God opened a door and found a teaching job for me.

23

Back Home Again — To Seattle

SEATTLE WAS FAMILIAR territory although the changes that time brings were obvious. Some buildings and businesses were gone. The confusion of new one-way streets was evident. New street and avenue names were everywhere.

The old neighborhoods still held memories as we traveled back in time.

We lived in a part of town I was not familiar with, and Allen went to a new junior high school called Worth McClure.

I got a job teaching at T.T. Minor Elementary School. It was in the "Hood"! I was made to feel quite welcome, and teaching there was a pleasure.

One day the daily paper had an article about the students at Allen's school. Allen was quoted as saying, "If I had my way, I wouldn't be going to school in the Queen Anne Area, I would be going to school in the hood!" I received many comments about my son's interview that day. You could count on Allen to say exactly what he thought, about anything.

We renewed our relationship with Barnetta and her husband Faniel, Byron and Alyne and all the children and grandchildren. It was a great time of sharing for us.

Reverend and Mrs. Solomon Hill were at First A.M.E. Church, and we became part of that fellowship.

Reverend and Mrs. Dorsey McCullough were there working with Reverend Hill, and they too became part of our extended family.

Faniel and Barnetta with their daughter Alyce — Barnetta ("Bita") was my first friend, and we were very close until the day she died.

These were friendships that were very special. Tessie Hill is still one of my dearest friends, and conversations with her are wonderful.

We were not too far from the Aurora Bridge, and Allen enjoyed fishing there. Everett and Theresa did their own thing and moved on in their pursuit of higher education.

Everett, as usual, did well in school. I was active in the Women's Missionary Society.

After a year Everett had finished his work and was ready to resume his pastoral duties.

24

Santa Ana — A Diamond in the Rough

THE BISHOP ASSIGNED Everett to Santa Ana, California. He and Allen went ahead, and I finished out my semester.

I had been blessed to have a student teacher, Althea Colvin, and I convinced my principal to hire her in my place, and she did. It was a challenge for Althea, but she did well.

Everett and I started looking for an apartment for me, but we were not impressed with anything that we saw.

Reverend and Mrs. Hill finally said, "You're coming home with us and then we won't have to worry about you."

Again God was in the plan, and I became one of the family. It was a beautiful three months for me. I was able to visit Allen and E.P. on holidays.

On one of my short visits to Santa Ana, I had an interview with the personnel director of the Santa Ana School District. It was a delightful session. He was impressed with my language skills and my record as a teacher. He said he wished he could have spent more time talking to me.

There was a special program there called the Language Development Center, where he felt I would really fit in. The purpose of the program was to help Spanish-speaking children to learn English as a second language.

This was the beginning of a teaching career that would last 14 years. I knew that God was in the plan once again because this was a time when teachers were not being hired in large numbers.

Everett certainly was "sent" to Johnson Chapel, "for just such a time as this." He was busy in the church, busy in the community, and still had time to be an excellent husband and father.

There were many opportunities for me to speak. I was busy and I loved it.

God always sent beautiful people into our lives.

I cannot name them all, for it would take another book, but those who had an lasting effect on our family were Carolyn Slaughter (now Carolyn Burns), Janice Bell Jackson, "who could open heaven's gate" when she sang, and Pat Davis who team-taught with me. Pat and Carolyn rescued me in my attempts to work artistically and showed me how to keep my bulletin boards pretty and up to date.

One Sunday an entire family of 17 joined our church, the Alaman family. They were spiritual warriors, and to this day the remaining members of the clan can be counted on to hold me up in prayer. Sister Ruby Wright and her family are yet my mentors, and when I have a special need they go down in prayer.

It was in Santa Ana that Everett first asked me to be his Sunday school superintendent. He did not place me in leadership capacities in the church, so I was honored and humbled. Our Sunday school was well established, and we kept a loyal staff on board. It was my first attempt in a supervisory position, and God truly blessed all of us.

While we were in Santa Ana, we discovered that Carol Austin Gordon, her husband Richard and their children were members of the church. What a wonderful reunion we had! They brought art and literature and helped out immeasurably in the Sunday school.

The church was housed in a very small building on the corner of Second and Bristol. The congregation had grown by leaps and bounds, and the need for a new church was evident.

Talking and planning began in earnest, and we had

RELIGION

Johnson Chapel Dedicates New Sanctuary

by Wayne Rash

"I'm a long ways from where I've been, but I gotta keep movin' till I push on in."

With those words sung by their junior choir filling the building, the members of Santa Ana's Johnson Chapel African Methodist Episcopal Church celebrated the dedication of their new sanctuary May 4.

The dedication service was a spirited conclusion to the many years of planning and preparation that resulted in the construction of the $310,000 facility on the southwest corner of 2nd and Bristol.

Directly across the street from the new building is the old sanctuary which had been used from 1947 until February of this year. The older building had been a military chapel at El Toro before its acquisition by the Johnson Chapel congregation.

Founded in 1933, Johnson Chapel is the city's second oldest black church. Its current pastor, Rev. Everett P. Williams, has served the church since 1970. During that period the membership has risen from 50 to almost 300 families.

In addition to the junior choir, the dedication service featured selections by the adult and youth choirs and greetings from several other AME congregations in southern California.

Keynote speaker was the AME district bishop. Rev. H. Hartford Brookins.

A frontal view of the new sanctuary, facing on Second Street west of Bristol Street.   *(Santa Ana Journal staff photo)*

Vernon Napier, vice-chairman of Johnson Chapel's Trustee Board, presents Bishop H. Hartford Brookins with the keys to the new sanctuary. Presiding Elder Paul Kidd stands between Napier and the bishop. To the bishop's right are Rev. Everett P. Williams, pastor of Johnson Chapel, and Samuel Baldwin, vice-chairman of the church Steward Board.   *(Photo courtesy of Johnson Chapel)*

Building the new church —
Praise God from whom all blessings flow!

the usual pros and cons. But God had his own plans and timetable.

After ten years of labor, the new Johnson Chapel was built right across the street.

Everett had reached the crowning point of his career in ministry. He had relocated a church, bought a parsonage with the help of God's people and a strong faith in a God who was able.

When the church was ready for occupancy, Everett Jr. came home to be his father's first Minister of Music in the new church.

Everett Jr. developed a choir, some of whose members are still active today. He got a job at the old Fundamental school. This was unusual because I was teaching at the brand new Fundamental school.

Everett Jr. stayed two years, and what a choir we had! I can still hear Janice Bell, Tina, Pam Jones, Valdoris Scott, Ruby Wright, Joyce Thorton, Edmond Williams and others who sang "Til earth and heaven met." Brothers Baldwin and Fant, Sister Laverene Washington, Marcellus and Mattie Lang, and Herbert Williams and others were important faithful officers of the church.

While we were in Santa Ana, Theresa completed her Masters Degree and came home with a beautiful baby daughter, Kamilah Madelyn.

Allen matriculated at Grambling University where he was an honor student, and Everett had served two years as head of the Music Department at Allen University.

Everyone in the family had a Masters Degree but me, so it was my turn.

Pepperdine University had a center in Orange County, and it only took 11 months to complete it. So here I was back in school and worked and received a Master of Science in Education.

Everett had done a good day's work at Johnson Chapel, and then he sensed it was time to move on.

Kamilah Madelyn, our first grandchild.

Kamilah and her proud grand-daddy!

25

Fresno, California

F RESNO, CALIFORNIA, "THE Raisin capital." Warm days, cool nights, hot summers.

No sooner than we arrived, we discovered that we would have to negotiate for a place to live.

A young steward, Rita Walker, offered us a sanctuary in her lovely home. It was just a blessing. Rita was active in the church and hospitable in her home.

It became apparent that she would become like an "adopted daughter." I remember planning and preparing the evening meal, and after dinner Rita and I would take long walks together.

With the help of trustee Sister Addie Rodgers, who managed the church-run housing project, we found a beautiful house and were able to purchase it as a parsonage.

Since the church bought the house, Everett and I agreed to buy our own furniture. Rita was adept at interior decorating, and she did a masterful job of making the house beautiful. She urged me to do one room, under her watchful eye; it was the master bathroom.

During this tenure of service, I accepted my second Conference Branch job. Conference Branch president. I had never even been a local president, but I asked God to make me a president, and he blessed the work. Rita became my secretary and my right hand, and what a tremendous help she was. I knew that she would at some time reach the top and, praise God, she did! She eventually became Conference Branch president of the California Conference. Ultimately she became a "preacher's wife."

Everett was behind me all the way, encouraging, supporting and helping me with technical problems associated with being a Sunday school superintendent and Conference Branch president.

While we served in Fresno, Reverend and Mrs. Norris Williams, who were pastoring in Fowler, California, stopped by on their way back to Livermore where they lived. They shared their gifts of fresh produce with us and became wonderful friends to this day.

Perhaps the most significant event for us while in Fresno was the celebration of our 40th wedding anniversary. The children felt that we should have it, because the 50th was still ten years away, and we had no idea where we would all be then.

The celebration was awesome. It was a very, very hot day, but we had a grand time.

There were people from southern California, Oakland, Stockton, Berkeley and other places. People we had worked

Repeating our vows after 40 years — Rev. John R. Thornton and twin brother Edward officiating.

The family celebrating Blanche and Everett's 40th anniversary. (L-R): Lydia Brown (niece), Kamilah, Everett, Blanche, Mabel Olivier (cousin), Theresa, Everett Jr.

with, grown up with and friends we had made in ministry attended. The children "out-did" themselves.

My teaching career was actually a wonderful learning experience. I worked with physically challenged children who were being mainstreamed into regular classrooms. I had about five the first year.

I had a wonderful principal, Dr. Alan Harrison. Teaching for me had proven to be a God-sent career. Dr. Harrison was to have spoken at our anniversary celebration. He was not able to attend, but the following letter he sent seemed to be an earthly validation of the fact that part of my desire to be different showed itself in my approach to the job.

Everett and Blanche — a fitting end to the ceremony.

Blanche and Rev. Williams, may I express my regrets for not being able to attend the celebration of this most important occasion for both of you.

I have been asked to say a few words about Blanche Williams, the teacher. However, it is impossible to describe one's role as a teacher without first looking at that person as an individual — how he or she governs his/her life and the code by which that individual lives. Blanche Williams is among the most noble and honorable of all the people I have ever met. Her strong faith in God and her strong moral convictions leave no question about her life's priorities. Her obvious love for her fellow man and her strong belief in hard work and dedication to task are readily apparent. She is a person without guile — one whose strong Christian beliefs are ingrained in everything that she does.

With this now understood, I can discuss Blanche Williams, the teacher.

To separate a teacher's personal life from his/her professional life is an impossibility (although there are those who believe it can be done easily). To be an effective teacher, one must be those things which Blanche Williams is. One must have a strong sense of justice, a strong moral code, a love of mankind and a willingness to work hard. A teacher must be dedicated to those around him/her and see the good in people — their strengths — and work to improve those characteristics which need attention.

Blanche has great respect for her students and a profound sense of the important charge she has been given. Her focus is directed by a sense of a long future and a sense of the eternal nature of our existence. She is concerned not only with how well a student learns to read, but how well that student will adapt to society and how well that student will accept himself. She is concerned with the type of citizen her students will become and the type of parents they will become. In short, Blanche is dedicated to working with the "whole child and views her task as a global one.

I have missed working with Blanche these past several months. I fully realize the importance of her present calling and look forward to the time when we are again able to work together. Blanche — you are THE BEST! May the future hold many, more wonderful and productive years for you. Congratulations on your 40 years of marriage and 35 years as an educator. Congratulations on raising such fine children who care so much about both you and your husband. You have contributed so much — and we all love you very much.

Blanche, every word is from my heart!

Alan Harrison, 9/17/86

Letter from Dr. Alan Harrison, my principal in Fresno. He wanted to wish us well for our 40th anniversary.

Everett and I were blessed to be able to take pride in the jobs that each of us was called to do.

Everett's twin brother Edward was one of those whose encouragement early on was helpful in my decision to take the teaching job.

Later Edward and Mary found their place in our lives. They reared together two fine chil-

dren, Paul and Gwennie, and now Mary moves on without Ed, but is devoted stepmother and doting grandmother.

As my sisters in ministry will discover, time goes swiftly and the time comes to leave friends and challenges and move on to new tasks.

The twin and his wife — Edward and Mary Williams. Mary and I enjoy a good fellowship in the absence of our soul mates.

26

Arizona — A New Frontier

T UCSON, ARIZONA PRESENTED itself as a new frontier for us, a different kind of weather and another view of our United States.

Again, housing was the first real test. The parsonage had been a lovely place to live in, but its time was running out. After more than 40 years in the work, I really felt that it was time to be assertive and live in an up-to-date home. It was here where I really understood how "sacred" parsonages are to the members. There are people who remember when it was built or purchased, people who remember babies born to the pastoral family. There are memories that they have of making repair after repair. I learned to respect that! I also felt that church members must learn to see the other side and come to want their first family to be comfortable and happy.

We looked for a place, and God sent us to Johnnie and Jerry Majors who accepted us while we looked.

We had so much fun with the Majors. They were a kind and loving couple.

I remember the bowling nights. Before they left, Jerry would cook his famous steaks for dinner. Oh, they were so tender and good! With the baked potato and broccoli, we would all feast.

We played dominoes together, too. I remember that Johnnie said "she had no idea of what Pastors and their wives went through." We stayed with them until the Lord provided a brand-new house for us. We were so happy and couldn't wait for the day when I could cook the whole meal

Sisters in Christ — Naomi Shaw and Blanche

for them in my kitchen.

I continued to speak for special occasions, and Everett was always there to encourage me. He really listened!

It was during this pastorate when in 1988 I joined our oldest son, Everett Jr., and the Shiloh Baptist Church family of Washington, D.C. on a pilgrimage to the Holy Land.

Everett Sr. spent the time with other members of the family, as he didn't really feel he could go. I will never forget that trip.

We renewed our friendship with Reverend and Mrs.

Just having a special night with the Victoria family — Bill and Louise, Everett and Blanche.

Victoria meets the U.S. — Bernice with Everett Jr. Good times!

Victoria is always so much fun. Front: Ray Mitchell, Margaret Louise. Back: Muz Scotney, Elizabeth (Betts) Dunkeley.

The Canadian family, Sooke, B.C. — home of Donna and Lloyd.

John Shaw who were at Tanner A.M.E. Church in Phoenix. We had some wonderful times together.

My relatives, Bill, Louise, Bernice, Margaret, Ray, Betts and Muzz, from Victoria, British Columbia, came to visit us one summer. What a time we had!

27

Take Me Back To Where
We Started — The Midwest

Everett WAS SOON sent to Gregg Tabernacle A.M.E. Church in Kansas, Missouri.

Our nephew, Edward P. Williams, Jr., had pastored this church and, in fact ,was called home to be with the Lord while there. Everett did not see this as a deterrent to his being there, so he accepted the appointment.

Everett and I were able to enjoy seeing old friends again and spent time reminiscing about our times together in days past.

We were not able to get into the parsonage right away, so were invited to stay with Reverend Ron Williams and his wife Vivian until remodeling and renovations were completed. To this day Vivian and her family remain a dearly beloved part of my family.

The work at Gregg Tabernacle provided opportunities for "in-house" gatherings. There had been several pastors who did not stay long, so relationships need to be restored.

Everett was very busy, and our work thrived. I helped out in the office and particularly in the Sunday school and Missionary Society.

We saw our young people grow and become a more visible part of the church.

On of the beautiful things that happened to us when we got to Kansas City was the joy of seeing relatives on my father's side. We were now somewhat near Aunt Dot, Mabel, Audrey and Warrick and Barbara. Mabel had spent some time with us while we were in Santa Ana, California, but then she later returned to Wichita where the others were.

Our visits there were always pleasant and enjoyable.

Warrick Milton, Cynthia and the girls, Ericka and Jennifer lived in Overland Park, so we could see each other a bit more often, usually at a church service.

After the first year and a half we moved from the parsonage to our own home in Grandview, Missouri, the city where I still live today.

I worked on the Conference Branch Missionary Society, under the leadership of Jeri Morris who became a sister and friend. I also worked in the local Society under the inspired leadership of Mary Agnes Brown. Mary Agnes became a real friend and stood with us in all of our efforts to keep the work going. Along with Aurora Winn, they became our prayer partners.

Milo and Plum Mitchell were like extended family and could be counted on wherever they were needed. Periodically we ate out together.

Space will not allow me to mention others who were so much a part of our ministry there. The Abney family was among those who were most loyal.

Eventually, Everett felt that it was time to ask for a lighter work, so when an opening was available we went to St. Paul, Kansas City, Kansas.

We had begun our journey in Olathe, Kansas at St. Paul, and it turned out that we would end our pastoral life at St. Paul, Kansas City, Kansas.

28

Everett's Retirement

AT THE ANNUAL Conference held in Topeka, Kansas, at St. John, Everett told me he had something to tell me. I wanted to know right away what was on his mind, so I followed him to a quiet place. He said, "The Lord had spoken to him saying it was time to retire."

I said, "Whatever you do is okay with me."

When he told Bishop Anderson, the Bishop was saddened because he knew Everett to be an humble and obedient servant of the Lord.

At that very conference in 1994, Everett and three other pastors were granted retired status.

We joined Christ Our Redeemer, which was closest to our home.

Reverend Timothy and Maureen Tyler were like our own children, and we were able to continue a relationship which had begun before God called Timothy. We rejoiced with them when their daughter, Imani, was born and later when God blessed them with a son, Chinelo.

Christ Our Redeemer was a warm and friendly church, and we were welcomed with open arms. We came to know many of them as "family." We couldn't mention all of them, but among those we'll never forget are: Brother Roy Walker, Sister Gloria Watson, Mother Darlene Bailey, Wanda Richberg, Marguerite Davis and Carolyn Strickland.

As happened so often in the itinerant ministry, Timothy's work there was completed, and he was sent to Johnson Chapel, Santa Ana, California.

Reverend Ronnie McCowan was sent as pastor to

Christ Our Redeemer and brought the very sweet "First Lady" Carolyn and daughters, Roshanda and Brianna.

29

A New Lifestyle

ONE DAY EVERETT was sitting in the living room very quietly. I came in and saw that he didn't look well.

He had seen Dr. Lee two days before. He had had pneumonia. She had told him if after two days he wasn't better, he needed to call her. Dr. Lee was very attentive and always answered her calls immediately. I told her how he looked and felt, and she said, "Take him to the hospital now!"

I called Reverend McCowan, our pastor, to see if he could come right over and take him, and he said yes. He had the girls with him, and he dropped them off to dance class on the way to pick us up to take us to the hospital.

When we arrived at the Independence Regional Hospital, we got a wheel chair, and I wheeled Everett into Emergency. The staff worked with him only a few minutes and said that he was to be admitted.

Several doctors were called in, and I was told not to leave because they didn't expect him to make it through the night. I called our children and suggested they wait until I knew more. Needless to say, they all came anyway.

I was doing pretty well until I saw Bobbi Lucas, and the tears almost came. Bobbi and Luke were our fishing partners, and we shared many good times together. She loved E.P. and was willing to do anything for us.

It was touch and go with Everett.

Warrick Milton, the A.M.E. clergy, and many, many friends came to support us. Denise Hunter spent the night with me at the hospital, and the hospital provided a special room for us because so many had come to be with us. They had placed Everett on a ventilator.

I remember Reverend Raymond Handy walking down the corridor with me one afternoon. I asked him what he thought, and he said, "I think that he's crossing over."

When I saw the doctors again, I said, "I want you to take him off the ventilator. I will never know what God can do until I give him a chance." The doctors were very concerned and told me all of the dangers such a move could mean, even death.

I insisted, and the next afternoon they turned everything off. Praise God, after all, God is in charge.

After a brief stay in Skilled Nursing, I took my beloved Everett home. Later when we were talking about his illness, I told him, "I don't know how I had the courage to ask to have you taken off the ventilator." He said, "It was your faith in God that led you to make your decision, and God honored your faith."

Everett Jr. came back home to help me with his dad for a short while. With our loving care, Everett was nursed back to a reasonable measure of health.

His energy level was not high, and it was frustrating not to be able to do the work he had always taken such pride in doing. He did teach me how to do a few things like shining our shoes and waxing the floor, but still preferred that I not do the housework. The maintenance of a large home was not working for us, and so while we could make our own decisions we put the house up for sale and moved into the new Senior Citizen complex called Truman Farm Villas, where I still live today.

Reverend McCowan had moved on and was succeeded by Reverend Ralph Crabbe. Reverend Crabbe had been dutiful in visiting Everett and was kind in his treatment of a retired pastor.

30

God's Plan for Everett

I BEGAN TO sense that Everett needed a more seasoned pastor who understood all the spiritual needs of a retired shepherd. We talked to Reverend Crabbe and agreed that Reverend Raymond Handy at St. John A.M.E. Church in Kansas City, Missouri would be the right choice.

We joined the St. John family and stayed there where Everett enjoyed his last ministerial home.

Reverend Handy was excellent in caring for Everett's spiritual needs and proved to be a brother beloved.

Allen and his dad at Bethel. A beautiful, bonding family togetherness happened here!

We developed a very special relationship with both Reverend Handy and his devoted wife, Euna Marie. Euna and I called each other often, and she provided comfort and support for me.

At the mid-year conference our son, Allen, was sent to pastor Bethel A.M.E. Church in Kansas City, Missouri.

I believe that one of the most beautiful seasons in Everett's life came as he watched Allen grow and follow in his footsteps in the ministry.

Everett enjoyed worshipping with him at Bethel, participating in the service whenever he could.

I recall the last Sunday when Everett tried to assist his son in administering the Holy Communion.

After service was over and we were getting into our car to go home, he said, "I just made it during Communion. If the table hadn't been there for me to hold onto, I couldn't have remained standing." He was "trying to tell me." He was nearing the end of the journey, but I still didn't get it!

31

The Fabulous Fiftieth Anniversary

THE FIFTIETH ANNIVERSARY, August 24th, 1998, was an outstanding event that can only be categorized as "special," and it stands alone.

Our 50th Anniversary, August 1996, at Bethel A.M.E. Church, with the whole family gathered around.

An Anniversary Prayer

Our gracious loving heavenly Father, the Creator and sustainer of life, thank you for bringing us together over 50 years ago. Now as we celebrate our Golden Wedding Anniversary, we humbly acknowledge that we have come this far by faith. Lord, you have guided us with your spirit, protected us with your might, surrounded us with your love, kept us through your grace, and blessed us with your mercy. Than, you for making possible this celebration for us. Thank you for our children; thank you for our grandchildren; thank you for our relatives and for our mighty host of dear friends. We pray that you, Lord, will continue to keep us in the center and circle of your love through Him who does all things well, even Jesus Christ our Lord.   Amen.

— Reverend Everett P. Williams, Sr.

32

The Next Five Years

AFTER EVERETT'S VERY near fatal illness, we began to look at life in a different way. We did everything together. Shopping, attending church and other meetings, if you saw one, you saw the other.

I put my life and desires on hold for him. No more trips for anything. No more delegate status for anybody.

It was my joy to be there for him. We used to sit together holding hands. It was as though we were courting all over again.

Our last trip to Victoria was so very pleasant. One day we were visiting cousins who were camping. Everett and Cousin Bill Ross went for a walk. When they came back, Everett was exhausted. He said, "I almost didn't make it." He was trying to tell me that he wouldn't be here a lot longer, but I didn't get it.

We went to North Carolina to see Theresa and Willie's new home. He blessed it for them. It was a beautiful visit. We laughed as Everett checked everything out and tried to make sure that they listed everything for the final walk-through.

We visited Everett Jr., as he was to perform with the Washington Performing Arts Society, "Children of the Gospel Mass Choir." He was a guest music director at the Kennedy Center.

He was very thrilled because Jennifer Holiday was the special guest artist. He directed "Ave Maria," "Holy Is the Lamb" and, as a special number, they did excerpts from "I Have a Dream," Dr. Martin Luther King, Jr. "We Shall Not

Willie and Theresa Wilkes' new home — Everett was able to bless it for them.

be Moved," an opera by Everett P. Williams, Jr. Included was the section, "My Brothers and My Sisters."

This was indeed a very special time for us. We were to know later just how special these times were, after we got home.

We were Willie and Theresa's first guests.

33

Dealing With a Life-Threatening Illness

UPON OUR RETURN home from visiting Everett, the beginning of our long ordeal began. Everett and I had gone to the office of our complex to take care of some business and were returning to our apartment. When we got back into our apartment, Everett went into our back bedroom to hang up his jacket. He called to me and said, "I just did hang up my jacket and I can hardly make it!"

I said, "Can you come out here and sit down?" I helped him and I could see that he was stressed out. His heart was beating fast, and I said, "We had better call 911." He didn't want me to, but I insisted. The paramedics came and checked him out and asked him if he wanted to go to the hospital, but he really didn't. Sharon Acton, who used to work for us, saw the ambulance and came upstairs. Realizing who it was, she came in. Having had nursing experience, she knew we should go and she said, "Go, get to the hospital," and we did. We went to the nearest hospital that was St. Joseph's Hospital.

It was determined that he needed a heart-by-pass, and it was scheduled immediately. On the way to surgery he said to me, "Remember that I love you. I always have and I always will." I told him that I loved him, too.

34

Father and Son

D R. LEE ASKED the doctors to transfer him to our own hospital, Independence Regional Hospital, where our doctors served. Dr. Bowlin would see him every day.

The by-pass surgery was successful, but complications set in immediately afterwards, and then the longest most serious ordeal of his life was to take place.

The children were called to come and see their dad. The long vigil was difficult, but once again, good doctors, attentive nurses, a loving family and friends surrounded us.

Our beloved family — Kamilah Madelyn, Willie and Theresa.

Our beloved family —
Everett Jr.

Allen had a most diffi-
cult task of providing
spiritual nourishment
and giving comfort as a
son. He came to the hos-
pital every day and had
lunch with me and was
very strong.

We kept in touch with
Theresa and Everett Jr.
daily. I lived at the hospital and went home only
twice. It was all I could do.
Dr. Bowlin reminded me
that I should get some rest or I would end up in the same
hospital in another room. I knew he was right, but I just
couldn't leave Everett's side.

As I look back, I remembered that one day Everett and
I were sitting on the couch. Suddenly he looked at me and
said, "I might go before you. I know that I could never
make it without you, but you can make it without me."
Once again he was "trying to tell me," but I just didn't get
it!

All of our clergy friends came to the hospital. They were

just wonderful, supportive and caring. Lest I forget one, I'll forego naming them.

They prayed with us, brought gifts and offered any support we needed.

Our beloved family — Allen Louis, Meryl Ashley, Marcheta and Allen Louis Sr.

35

Glimpses of the Journey's End

ONE AFTERNOON, REVEREND and Mrs. Handy and Reverend and Mrs. Finnell were with me at the hospital. We were sitting in the waiting room. Both families were so loving and kind. We suddenly heard over the intercom, "Code Blue," and the sound of people rushing. I said, "I'm glad they aren't going in Everett's direction." I got up to look and see, and suddenly I realized that they had gone into his room. The nurse came out and said it had happened so quickly, but they brought him back. We had requested in writing that Everett's status would be "DNR" (Do Not Resuscitate), but I was not in the room to enforce it. I know now that it was not to have been his last moment.

I had prayed to God that should he go, I only wanted to be there with him. Once again, I realized that God was in the plan.

Each day I had devotions with him in his room. I prayed with him and read scripture. The nurses gave me a space in his room to write the verse of the day where he could see it.

Everett told me that he was at the gate waiting. I asked if he was waiting for Jesus and he said "yes."

Presiding Elder Carolyn Guidry came to see him one afternoon. Everett had also told me that the waters were parting. I asked the Elder what she thought he meant, and she said, "He's crossing the Jordan." I understood what she said, but I still couldn't get it. He was trying to tell me.

Very soon after that conversation, I had gone home. I checked our mail, changed clothes and got a few more things done at home. I went to bed early and actually had a good night's sleep.

The next morning I got up and made preparations to drive to the hospital. As I drove, I sang to myself almost all the way. I was singing, "I Come to the Garden Alone," all the way to the hospital.

Later in a conversation with my cousin, Reverend Warrick Graves, he told me that on that same morning, he too was singing the same song at approximately the same time that I was.

When I drove into the hospital parking lot, I sensed that this was no ordinary day. It was April 17, 2001.

I went straight to Everett's room. He had been moved to a private room because the doctors and nurses thought a change of scenery might help him to recover.

They were waiting for a bed in the rehabilitation unit of the hospital.

I did not want him to go because the therapy treatment was so traumatic and he fought it. God was in the plan, and the nurse said, "Mrs. Williams, you don't have to worry, no bed is available."

It was very serene and peaceful in his new room. When I got there, he was calm and happy to see me. He held out his hand for me to hold. He asked for a drink, but all they would give him was a spoonful of ice. I had only allowed them to use the oxygen mask, so they removed it so he could accept the ice. When they tried to put the mask back, he summoned enough strength to move it away.

I held his hand and asked the nurse to please let him alone. We just looked lovingly at each other. I knew then what he tried so often to tell me. He was going to leave me and go home to be with his Heavenly Father. I could almost envision him in heaven.

I told him how very much I loved him. I said. "You are tired and you are ready to go and be with the Lord. It's all right, you earned it."

I knew if it was going to happen, it would be very, very soon. I could see tears beginning to form in his eyes.

Then I said, "And I'm letting you go." I had finally "gotten it!" At that moment, Everett tilted his head back, laid it on the pillow and closed his eyes.

The nurse said, "I've never seen it like this. This is awesome, he waited for you."

Yes, he had tried so hard to tell me, and he waited until "I got It."

At 10:15 a.m., April 17, 2001, the Incredible Journey on this side of heaven was over.

36

People, Places and Things
To Be Cherished Forever

EVERETT WAS A gifted singer and enjoyed doing it immensely. He sang everything, as he had had voice training as a young man.

Early in his youth, he, his twin brother Edward and a couple of their cousins formed a quartet and sang at the old Palomar Theater in Seattle, Washington.

When I first met him, he was on a program to sing, and I was amazed. I knew right away that he could sing for me forever.

When he preached, you could always count on a song before or after the sermon.

I still listen to the tapes made in family gatherings. He loved to sing "He Knows Just How Much You Can Bear," "Balm In Gilead," "It Took a Miracle" and "He Touched Me."

Music was part of our family. He loved to hear our niece, "Babee," sing "O Holy Night" and "He's got the Whole World in His Hands."

All of our family gatherings revolved around a good meal, laughter and jokes and singing. I guess Al and I were the only two who didn't sing.

Al was Babee's husband. They had one talented daughter, Lydia Ruth. At several of our family gatherings we shared time with Dorothy and her children, Brent and Shanee. Edward Jr. passed away in 1981, and Dorothy devoted herself to raising the children, and what a tremendous job she did!

There were the fun songs that Everett taught the children. We all got a big bang out of hearing them sing, "Oh

Mister, Mister Johnny Forbeck" and "Sweet Rosie O'Grady."

I tried to get him to teach the songs to Meryl and Allen II, but he wouldn't. He said they would probably sing them in church! And their mom, Marcheta, said they probably would have.

Everett was full of rhythm, and when just the two of us were alone, he would dance for me. I really enjoyed watching him and would just laugh and laugh. He said, "You get such a charge out of this!" I really, really did.

I asked him to teach me some steps. He laughed and said, "Honey, I can't teach you, you don't have any rhythm." He was right, I didn't!

There was never a Sunday morning as we were ready to leave for church that he failed to tell me how good I looked. "It didn't matter which outfit I wore, he liked it!" I thought he looked very smart, well-groomed and handsome. And I told him so.

I shall always remember his prayers. He prayed like he lived. He gave it everything he had. I'm sure he made contact with God every time he prayed. He was always being asked to pray at community gatherings, church and always led prayer time at home.

Family devotions were the foundation and cornerstone of our lives. I do believe the children became very good readers because they took turns reading scripture and the *Upper Room* at morning devotions at home.

Everett was a very early riser and had his own personal devotions long before anyone was up.

I recall that one of his favorite poems was "I Met God in the Morning."

When Ed came to visit us or we went to visit him, the twins would have coffee and Bible study as early as three or four o'clock in the morning. It was a habit for Everett during the entire 54 years of our marriage.

I believe this ritual of family devotions was one of the

finest legacies he left his children. Families that don't pray together and read the Bible together miss a wonderfully intimate family time.

Everett was my best critic and fan. He didn't mind listening to my messages as I prepared them and then hearing me deliver them.

The very last message he heard me deliver was entitled, "Angels or Strangers." On our way home, he said, "That's the best I've ever heard you." That message was actually the very last one I delivered.

As a Bible study teacher, he was terrific. His Bible studies were a very rich experience. He was tough, but enjoyable. He would sometimes listen to your opinions, but when you finished, he would say, "But what does the Bible say?" He made sure you understood the word. He was a "no-nonsense" teacher. He made the word come alive.

In the last months of his life, he often told me, "I think a lot about Ed these days."

I'm sure now that these moments were also moments when "he tried to tell me that he wasn't going to be here long."

My sister-in-law, Mary, and I have shared conversations about the twins, and some of her experiences paralleled mine.

I remember Shirley and Paul and the relaxing times at their ranch. We fished for breakfast and we took long walks.

I was not the finest cook in the world, but he seldom missed an opportunity to thank me for his meals.

However, I recall a time in Oakland, California, when I tried a new dish. He looked at me with that "twitch" of the lip and said, "You don't need to cook this anymore." I answered quickly, "If you don't like it, you can get up from the table!" He really did, and his three loyal children followed him. Later we had many laughs over that little episode.

He was loving, kind and gentle and so appreciative of all I did for him and the children.

He never let them forget that many of the special treats they got were because Mama worked.

I often think of the fun that we had playing Scrabble and dominoes together. We had fun and never got tired of playing.

Everywhere we went, we found "children and young people." Our extended family was large.

In our last years together in Kansas City, we were Grandma Williams to Jonquilyn Hill, Roshanda, Brianna and Aaron McCowan; Aunt Blanche to Imani and Chinelo Tyler, D'Andrea and Ronald Williams.

One of the greatest blessings was being around our own grandchildren here, Meryl and Allen. This was special, because we had been close to Kamilah when she was their age.

Of very special note was our relationship as Mom to Juli and Glendal Whitney and "Aunt" Williams to Glendal II, Grant, Amanda and Garrison. Watching Juli, whom I first met as a baby and then mature as a licentiate for ministry, has been exciting. God has truly directed our paths.

Speaking of young people we helped and nurtured, we were very fond of Essie Lena Parker. She often baby-sat for us, and I'll never forget how she hated to see us punish our children, especially the spankings. She told us, "When she has children she will never spank them." She later married Booker Lee, and they had two children. "We wondered if she changed her mind!"

On Easter Sunday, April 4, 2003, I read my daily little prayer card in a set given to me by Lucilla Miller, a Sunday school teacher at Bethel.

The card read. "For the Lord shall be thine everlasting light and the days of thy mourning shall be ended." Isaiah 60:20.

The preceding incidents are precious memories. Precious memories that will be with me the balance of my days lovingly remembered by me and shared with Everett Williams Sr.

I was also known by Everett as "Button-nose" and "My little Yabistraw."

37

I See Everett P. Williams, Sr.

WHEN I HEAR Theresa talk with her brilliant command of the English language and her unique way of using words. When she laughs with that hearty infectious tone. I hear Everett P. Williams in her voice.

When I watch Everett Jr. conduct and I notice the rhythm with which he moves, I see Everett P. Williams Sr. in him. And when he sings with resonance and feeling, it's like hearing his dad.

When I watch Allen move about in the congregation,

Theresa is very much like her dad — always laughing and speaking with authority and frankness.

The brothers, Everett Jr. and Allen — chips off the old block!

so thoroughly at home, and when I hear him preach, it's like hearing Everett Sr. The comments of the people responding to the wonderful way he conducts a funeral and delivers a eulogy — just like his Dad. I see Everett P. Williams Sr. in him.

As long as I live, their devotion to their father as reflected in their lives, "It will remind me of how special Everett was."